Simple Joys

TEXT BY *Claire Cloninger*

PAINTINGS BY *Michal Sparks*

HARVEST HOUSE PUBLISHERS

Eugene, Oregon

Simple Joys

Text Copyright © 2000 by Claire Cloninger
Published by Harvest House Publishers
Eugene, Oregon 97402

ISBN 0-7369-0337-2

Text is adapted from *A Place Called Simplicity* by Claire Cloninger (Harvest House Publishers, 1993).

Design and production by Garborg Design Works, Minneapolis, Minnesota

"The House We Call Home," from *Love Will Be Our Home*, lyric by Claire Cloninger/music by Keith Christopher, © Word Music, 1991.
"Elixir," © Robert A. Cloninger, 1984.
Anne Morrow Lindbergh, *Gift from the Sea* (New York: Pantheon, 1955), 114-115.
John Burroughs, quoted in David E. Shi, *In Search of the Simple Life* (Salt Lake City: Peregrine Smith Books, 1986), 192.
John Hadamuscin, *Simple Pleasures* (New York: Harmony Books, 1992), 7.
Wendell Berry, "II," *Sabbaths* (San Francisco: North Point Press, 1987), 8.
Claire Cloninger, "Precious Child," *Christmas Is Calling You Home* (Dallas: Word, 1997).

Contents

*With an eye made quiet by the power of harmony,
and the deep power of joy, we see into the life of things.*

WILLIAM WORDSWORTH

Believing

4

in Simplicity

Sweet Memories of Simple Joys

I think I had always believed in the existence of a place called Simplicity—a place where people could slow down and unravel the complications of their lives. I had spent vacations there and a few wonderful spiritual retreats. But, I wondered, could there really be an everyday kind of place like that—a place of quiet beauty and simple joy—where one could put down roots and stay?

It's More than a House, It's Home

Probably the quickest agreement my husband, Spike, and I ever came to on any subject was the day we first laid eyes on the beautiful, tranquil spot on the river that we now call home. It was love at first sight for the both of us. However, I didn't know at the time that what he saw in his mind's eye when he looked at this place was something quite different from what I saw. I saw a retreat where we could come now and then to untangle our busy lives and rest and be refueled to go back into our normal rat race. I saw a vacation getaway. But I believe Spike always saw a home.

If you are content, you have enough to live comfortably.

Titus Maccius Plautus

6

*Life's simplest
things are love, and
kindly friends,
Nature's sweet
charm of earth and
sea and sky;
Gladness of soul
that with right
living blends —
Home's dear
content, so cheap
that all may buy.*

RIPLEY D. SAUNDERS

Sweet Memories

In the summers of my early childhood, Simplicity was a town called Fishville. Our days there were remarkably the same. After breakfast we kids would splash in the creek, creating "playhouses" in the spindly roots of trees that lined its banks or building dams to create little "floating pools" or staging water-bug races. Later, after the adults were breakfasted and coffeed, we could usually persuade one of them to take us for a real "deep water" swim down at Cassan's Branch or up at Dean's Hole. After lunch everybody, regardless of age, napped while whirring fans stirred the summer air and the various-pitched snores of assorted uncles harmonized in a gentle, reassuring lullaby.

Safe and Happy

If I had to design a simple world, I'd be hard-pressed to find a better
model than Fishville, with its lazy, easy summer days and nights. I felt safe
there, and happy, and good about my world. I understood the rules (which
were few) and I knew I was loved (which was everything). So I think that for
years I blended my ideas of simplicity along
with my memories of Fishville into the same
sweet nostalgia soup.

Daydreaming

I smile now to remember all the summer evenings we'd sit out on the front porch by the river, daydreaming and wondering and idly talking about what it would be like to move out here permanently. Out here, Spike could garden and do carpentry and woodcarving and maybe even take up painting again. Out here, without the distractions of living in town, perhaps I could actually find time to write the novel I had always yearned to write. In this lovely, peaceful environment, maybe I could even win the war against my migraine headaches. And, of course I always pictured friends and family driving out for visits every weekend, for picnics and canoe rides and long, lazy conversations.

Within your heart, keep one still, secret spot where dreams may go.
LOUISE DRISCOL

The east bank of the road shelved suddenly. It dropped below him twenty feet to a spring.
The bank was dense with magnolia and loblolly bay, sweet gum and gray-barked ash.
He went down to the spring in the cool darkness of their shadows. A sharp pleasure came over him.
This was a secret and a lovely place.

MARJORIE KINNAN RAWLINGS
THE YEARLING

A Prayer of the Heart

Simplicity can begin for you as it did for me—as nothing more than an underground yearning, a prayer of the heart. This yearning can become a belief that becomes an attitude or a mindset that leads to a series of small choices that impel a series of small changes in the way we do things. And it is these small changes that finally (if diligently clung to) can begin to become a lifestyle.

Simplicity is more of an attitude than an agenda. Living in simple surroundings really has helped us simplify our attitudes as well.

CLAIRE CLONINGER

Your Own Journey

There is so much I want to share with you—ideas and insights that have changed my life and that I hope can open you up to a new ease and clarity and inner serenity. If you were here, we might sit out on our screen porch this evening and talk it over while the breeze blows off the river, while the night sounds of whippoorwills and frogs and crickets make background music and the moon rises and reflects in the water. If you like to read in bed, you could crawl up in our big four-poster and stay up as late as you like reading this book. Then you could sleep in tomorrow, because that's allowed here.

To the right, books; to the left, a teacup.
In front of me, the fireplace; behind me, the post.
There is no greater happiness than this.

TEIGA

A Green

Then the Lord God planted a garden in Eden, to the

east, and placed in the garden the man he had formed.

The Lord God planted all sorts of beautiful trees there

in the garden, trees producing the choicest of fruit.

THE BOOK OF GENESIS

Garden with a Good God

Simple Joys from Nature

The Original Plan

Sometimes after watching the evening news, I find myself thinking, "Surely things were never meant to be like this." I believe we were designed for something very different—something simple and sensible and lovely and right. We were designed to walk through a green garden with a good God, communing intimately with him in the cool of the day, trusting in his provision, marveling at his creation, and enjoying his friendship forever.

You have let me experience the joys of life and the exquisite pleasures of your own eternal presence.
THE BOOK OF PSALMS

It is important to keep seeing with our hearts what our eyes cannot see. Seeing the simple, serene lives he wants to give us. The unrushed, unstressed days of tranquility and peace that we yearn for but are not yet experiencing. It is important to keep making small, simplifying choices one at a time with his help.

A Bouquet of Days

I love days—rare, mysterious kinds of days—when I almost have the feeling that time has been suspended. They arrive unexpectedly, unbidden and unplanned. And when they do, it is almost as though I am lifted up and out of time on the wings of some lovely experience.

I remember a "time out of time" kind of day, an almost enchanted November afternoon years ago when my sister, Alix, and I sat under the moss-draped oaks on my uncle's lawn in Thibodaux, Louisiana, watching our four little boys play in the autumn leaves. The sky was wide and blue, the air was clear and cool, and our children were wild with the joy of being alive. Again and again they would fall backward into the high, soft piles of leaves, laughing hysterically and squealing each other's names: "André and Curt and Andy and Marc! André and Curt and Andy and Marc!" We found ourselves laughing along with them, laughing until our sides ached. We lay on our backs looking up through the thick, woven pattern of the

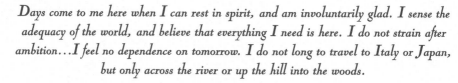

Days come to me here when I can rest in spirit, and am involuntarily glad. I sense the adequacy of the world, and believe that everything I need is here. I do not strain after ambition…I feel no dependence on tomorrow. I do not long to travel to Italy or Japan, but only across the river or up the hill into the woods.

WENDELL BERRY

branches and felt the closeness of heaven some- where behind the gentle blue covering of sky.

Through the years of my life other times like that have come to me as special gifts of grace: a nature hike at Girl Scout day camp when I was nine…my first big role in the school operetta…a ride on the Staten Island ferry with our children…a weekday afternoon at the mall with Spike and a couple of crazy pals, "playing hooky" from work…a holiday dinner with four women friends in front of a huge, blazing fire…an amazing Sunday of worship and fellowship with the body of Christ at the Brooklyn Tabernacle…a midnight vigil with Andy as we delivered a litter of mongrel pups…a picnic lunch with a dozen close friends on the grassy bald of a North Carolina mountain-top. What a joy to look back and gather up those lovely days like flowers for a bouquet.

The Heartbeat in Heaven

When I try to put words around an autumn afternoon like the one my sister and I spent with our children in the fallen leaves, I always have the feeling that our language lacks the needed words. There is no adequate way to describe or express in English the quality of a "time out of time" kind of time.

The Greek language is a little more helpful, however, because it has more than one word for time. *Chronos* is the Greek word for clock-controlled time. It describes the kind of time that is gauged by human measurement: by the hands of the clock and the pages of the calendar. Bills and term papers and taxes come due on *chronos* time. Monday mornings roll around with rigid regularity on *chronos* time. School, from the first day of first grade to the last diploma handed out on graduation day, runs on *chronos* time.

But there is another Greek word for what might be called "God-controlled time." That word is *kairos,* and it is the kind of time that we humans cannot gauge by clocks or calendars. With *kairos* time, God calls the shots. Flowers bloom on *kairos* time. Babies are born on *kairos* time. People fall in love and have spiritual awakenings on *kairos* time.

Kairos time is measured by "moments" rather than by minutes. We can't push it or force it or hold it back. It will only happen when a heartbeat in heaven has decided the time is right.

On a long-ago autumn afternoon, beneath the grandeur of spreading oaks, drenched in sunshine and squeals of laughter, I feel certain that my sister and I were watching our children on *kairos* time. What's more, I would venture to say that most of the deeply meaningful, memorable, difficult-to-describe moments that I hold close to my heart have been *kairos* moments in time.

The frog Philharmonic of the Florida lakes and marshes is unendurable in its sweetness.
I have lain through a long moonlit night, with the scent of orange blossoms
palpable as spilled perfume on the air, and listened to the murmur of minor chords
until, just as I have wept over the Brahms waltz in A flat on a master's violin,
I thought my heart would break with the beauty of it.

MARJORIE KINNAN RAWLINGS
CROSS CREEK

Joy All Around Us

It is a common misconception that "later on" we will finally be able to be happy—after a certain goal is reached or certain circumstances are changed. The simple truth is that happiness is a learned behavior and it takes most of us a lifetime to get the knack of it. There is only one time to begin learning how to appropriate the joy that is all around us, and that time is today!

No prisoners set at liberty could have felt more joy than we did as we stepped forth from our winter abode, refreshed our eyes with the pleasant verdure around us, and our ears with the merry songs of a thousand happy birds, and drank in the pure, balmy air of spring.

JOHANN DAVID WYSS
THE SWISS FAMILY ROBINSON

The House

I pass a lot of houses on my way home. Some pretty, some expensive, some inviting. But my heart always skips a beat when I turn down the road and see my house nestled against the hill.

BOB BENSON

We Call Home

Simple Joys at Home

Home Sweet Home

Loving a house is like any other kind of love. It is not a rational matter, but more a matter of the heart. Eventually our feelings will go beyond that first attraction. Deeper feelings will develop. If the times we have spent there have been mainly positive and nurturing, then our heart attitude and our feelings toward that place will be warm and good.

The simple home is a nurturing home. It is, literally and figuratively,
a safe and comfortable place to come in from the storms of life.

CLAIRE CLONINGER

The House We Call Home

It's just a house on a street in a town,
It may not look special to you,
But this is the house where we lived and we loved,
Where we slept and we ate and we grew.

CLAIRE CLONINGER

*He is the happiest, be he king or
peasant, who finds peace in his home.*

JOHANN WOLFGANG
VON GOETHE

28

Gracious Places

Simple homes are gracious places that have a ministry of their own in much the same way that people do. For example, the home of our friend Annie Hunt has a distinct ministry of joy. The wonderful, eclectic blend of furnishings, the colorful artwork, the framed photographs of Annie's children and grandchildren on every tabletop combine with the radiant personality of the hostess to present each guest with a gift of joy.

Susan and F.G. Baldwin's home has the ministry of prayer. Prayer in that home flows as easily as tap water! Many prayers go up from those beautiful, gracious rooms, and most of them are answered.

Our cabin has a ministry of rest and refreshment. People tend to drop their worry and compulsion up at the front gate, and by the time they travel the quarter mile to the house, their tension has begun to unwind.

The home of our friends Conlee and Signa has a wonderful ministry of fellowship. Their house is always filled with delicious smells from the kitchen and interesting guests. Good conversation and laughter are built into the times around their table.

A Precious Treasure

A home is truly a blessing, a treasure more precious than we realize. Whatever home we have been blessed to own or rent or otherwise inhabit is quite simply a gift, and the simple-hearted among us realize that good gifts are meant to be shared. Our homes should stand ready to welcome friends, kin, strangers, and pilgrims.

The Simplicity of Nature

Whether by way of a bountiful backyard vegetable garden, a flowerpot on a city windowsill, or even a beautiful landscape on the wall, almost every simple home has found a way to connect with nature. Simple homes exist in harmony with the creation of which they are a part. Simple homes are places where things and people bloom and grow side by side.

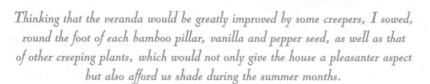

Thinking that the veranda would be greatly improved by some creepers, I sowed, round the foot of each bamboo pillar, vanilla and pepper seed, as well as that of other creeping plants, which would not only give the house a pleasanter aspect but also afford us shade during the summer months.

JOHANN DAVID WYSS
THE SWISS FAMILY ROBINSON

Elixir

Go amongst the waters here.
Shape yourself against the winds.
Measure their flow by your surfaces.
limb by liquid – skin by tempest,
Balm for the body.

Take on some golden here.
Bind yourself to purple and green.
Breathe deep of dark red and brown.
sunlight – petal – feather – leaf,
Salve for the spirit.

Fill your hollows with some music here.
Set your ear to its simple voices,
Resonant of change, a-hum with life.
sky and earth song – bird and brook song,
Medicine for the soul.

ROBERT A. CLONINGER

He did not live at all in the manner I had expected. I did not know much about his estate except that it was probably well over twenty thousand pounds, and I had expected to find my client living in a house with a servant or two. Instead, I discovered that he had a bedroom and a sitting-room on the same floor of a small private hotel just off the sea front.

NEVIL SHUTE
A Town Like Alice

Joyful

Unconcern

Simple Joys in Work

The simple life is always a life of
joyful unconcern for possessions.

RICHARD FOSTER

Blessed Space

When Spike and I cleaned out our house in Mobile in preparation for our move to the country, we made the decision to give away or sell much of what we owned, keeping only what we really needed (the essential) or highly treasured (the significant). It seemed that every closet and drawer and corner of the attic contained stacks of nonessential and/or insignificant things. Although I cannot say that this process of "stripping down" was easy or painless, I can tell you that it was tremendously liberating. As we pulled away from Mobile with only one small private mover's truck, I felt as if I had lost a thousand pounds. Actually, I had!

One rationale that helped me find the courage to get rid of excess baggage was this: I convinced myself that I was trading these possessions for something I treasured much more—space. Not only physical space, but spiritual and emotional space. The space I was gaining by decluttering brought with it a peace and serenity and simplicity that made parting with my things possible.

Anne Morrow Lindburgh made this acute observation about space:

It is only framed in space that beauty blooms. Only in space are events and objects and people unique and significant — and therefore beautiful. A tree has significance if one sees it against the empty face of the sky. A note in music gains significance from the silences on either side...Even small and casual things take on significance if they are washed in space.

To have what we want is riches, but to be able to do without is power.

GEORGE MACDONALD

The many things I parted with when I left Mobile have left a blessed space around the few things I have chosen to keep. For instance, I once had many china platters. Now I have one large one and one small one. Both are beautiful and special to me. They are essential for serving my food. And they are *significant* because they are the two I treasured enough to keep.

For my part, as I grow older, I am more and more inclined to reduce my baggage, to lop off superfluities. I become more and more in love with simple things and simple folk — a small house, a hut in the woods, a tent on the shore. The show and splendor of great houses, elaborate furnishings, stately halls, oppress me, impose on me. They fix the attention upon false values, they set up a false standard of beauty: They stand between me and the real feeders of character and thought.

JOHN BURROUGHS

Well-being is not defined by wealth, and so we can hold all things lightly — owning without treasuring, possessing without being possessed.

RICHARD FOSTER

Contentment is a
learned behavior.

CLAIRE CLONINGER

*I have learned how to
get along happily whether
I have much or little.
I know how to live on
almost nothing or with
everything. I have learned
the secret of contentment
in every situation, whether
it be a full stomach or
hunger, plenty or want.
For I can do everything
God asks me…*

THE BOOK OF PHILIPPIANS

*[The Amish] had shown me that any type of work can be meaningful.
It's the spirit in which you do it that makes the difference.*

SUE BENDER

Sweet Peace

Maybe your work moves at a sane, serene, and measured pace,
paying you just what you require for doing just what you enjoy.
Maybe you feel comfortable and satisfied
and fulfilled with what you do and the
hours you spend doing it and the
amount you are paid by the
people who need your services.
Maybe you can gaze proudly
at your finished product and
feel the sweet peace of a job
well done. Contentment with
your job situation is a wonderful, simple joy.

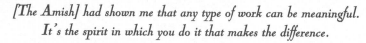

*To love what you do and feel that it matters —
how could anything be more fun?*

KATHERINE GRAHAM

Work hard and cheerfully at all you do, just as though you were working for the Lord…

<small>THE BOOK OF COLOSSIANS</small>

Add Joy

There is no more certain way to add joy to any task than to give it your all, continually reminding yourself that you are really performing for an "Audience of One." To seek the approval of human beings is to suffocate your soul, but to seek the approval of God is to breathe the pure air of his mercy.

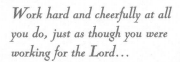

A sense of unity and simplicity comes from being who you are wherever you are.

<small>CLAIRE CLONINGER</small>

Seeking, Asking, Knocking

Simplicity is not necessarily linked to location. Moving into a log cabin won't suddenly make you simple, any more than moving into a college dorm will suddenly make you educated. Inner beliefs and commitments always have far more power to change our lives than any external move we can make. That is why I feel confident saying that if you really desire simplicity, if you are seeking, asking, and knocking, then the door to a simpler life will open to you.

But slowly I came to see that God desired to be not on the outskirts, but at the heart of my experience. Gardening was no longer an experience outside of my relationship with God — I discovered God in the gardening. Swimming was no longer just good exercise — it became an opportunity for communion with God. God in Christ had become the center.

RICHARD FOSTER

Slowing Down

Because I am an action person, my first inclination would be to rush to the starting line and begin cleaning out closets and cutting up credit cards. But I know by now that outward attempts to effect change rarely transform the inner person. Simplicity is not to move into a frenzy of activity, but rather to slow down.

Pockets of Apron

If I had only...forgotten future greatness and looked at the green things
and the buildings and reached out to those around me and smelled the air
and ignored the forms and the self-styled obligations and heard the rain
on my roof and put my arms around my wife...perhaps it's not too late.

HUGH PRATHER

Heaven on the of Earth

Simple Joys in Rest

Summer Simplicity

I grew up in a neighborhood of kids who really knew how to "do leisure." Summer afternoons after lunch, cooled by the churning of a huge attic fan, we'd suck on Kool-Aid ice cubes and read Nancy Drew mysteries. Summer evenings we'd play hide-and-seek or spotlight in our yard or the Morvants' until the air was thick and electric with "lightning bugs" and we could hear our moms calling names like verses in a familiar song, "Claire! Ann! Carolyn! Joanie! J.J.! Jeannie! Bobby! Time to come in!" After a bath and a goodnight kiss, we'd fall into bed, bone weary, and drift off to sleep thinking about what we'd play tomorrow.

One of my goals in moving to the country has been to relearn how to rest and recreate, to reclaim the ability to let go and enjoy my leisure and learn to feel good about times when I am not doing or achieving anything.

What to Do at a Log Cabin

Living in the country, I am finding fun and beauty, rest and recreation, in the most ordinary things. Just opening my eyes to what is around me, I am discovering a world of simple and relaxing pleasures.

For instance, blueberry and blackberry picking are among my spring and summer delights. Some mornings we just step out the back door and gather enough berries from our own bushes or vines to garnish our cereal bowls. When our friends or our children come out from town during berry season,

we equip them with bags and baskets and go on real "berry quests." What a wonderful setting for idle chatter among kindred spirits! And we always come home with the added bonus of baskets filled with ingredients for cobbler and homemade ice cream!

Gathering wildflowers and arranging them is another therapeutic and restful way to spend time here at Juniper Landing. Stargazing is yet another. Lying in the dark on a quilt and looking up into a million diamond

The ordinary arts we practice every day at home are of more importance to the soul than their simplicity might suggest.

THOMAS MORE

lights is a quiet and rejuvenating pastime—one that is available to many town-dwellers as well.

"Critter watching" is another restful country pleasure we don't take for granted. We have watched baby wrens hatching in a window box just outside our bedroom window. Raccoons, rabbits, deer, possums, and wild turkey are frequent guests at our little domain.

Other rest-inducing brands of recreation we enjoy are napping on rainy afternoons, gathering driftwood, making vine wreaths, and reading books aloud to one another. But perhaps the most enjoyable pastime for me at Juniper Landing is good dinner-table conversation when guests come from out of town. Something about this laid-back country setting seems to oil the wheels of conversation.

She woke many times throughout the night, and listened to the noises of the night, and watched the moonlight creep around the house, and she was happy.

NEVIL SHUTE
A TOWN LIKE ALICE

The happiest heart that ever beat
Was in some quiet breast
That found the common daylight sweet,
And left to Heaven the rest.

JOHN V. CHENEY

Rest Is a State of Mind

You don't have to go to the country to rest in simple ways. Most big cities are packed with things to do. You can stroll through museums, gaze at historical monuments, or stop at beautiful old churches where you can steal a quiet moment in midst of all the rush and noise. Years ago, when we lived in New Orleans, I would walk to the corner with baby Curt in tow and ride a streetcar just to get away for a while. I loved watching the people and taking in the sights, and Curt usually slept soundly in my arms to the rock and the rattle of the ride.

Every small town also has its own unique set of simple, noncompetitive, restful pleasures to be discovered and enjoyed: picnics, parades, local customs and crafts. Rest is truly not a function of where you live. It is a matter of shifting the way you think and allowing yourself to relax into the moment. So many forms of simple rest and recreation are available to almost anybody living almost anywhere: family time, evenings with friends, good books, playgrounds, romps with the dog, hobbies and crafts.

From the time we were small kids, my parents encouraged my brothers, my sister and me to take pleasure in those sweet and simple moments that can pop up on any old day, those moments that are sometime spontaneous, and never over orchestrated. As I've gotten older, and life continues to become more complicated and complex, I suppose I am just like everyone else — those simple things, those simple pleasures, continue to be what often make me most happy.

JOHN HADAMUSCIN

Sabbath Joy

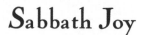

My husband has always been a hard worker, but he has always been good at letting his soul keep pace with his body. He is what I would call a world-class "rester." Spike's journal is full of his insightful Sabbath experiences. Here's a sampling from his "Juniper Journal":

A large grackle lands on a vine, almost within arm's reach, and studies me intently, cocking its head from side to side, peering at me first from one golden eye and then the other. As I slowly raise my camera this bird leaps with such a start that an autumn-browned leaf is knocked loose by its wing beat and the bird is out of sight before the loosened leaf lands on my shoe...I do love this place so. I feel the immediate presence of God in this October swamp...Surely today, this very day in October, he is passing through — perhaps as Grackle Companion. I am much blessed to have been here, too. I have had his leaf on my shoe.

The mind that comes to rest is tended

In ways that it cannot intend

Is borne, preserved, and comprehended

By what it cannot comprehend.

WENDELL BERRY

How good is man's life, the mere living!
How fit to employ all the heart and the soul and the senses forever in joy!

ROBERT BROWNING

*When we are truly in this interior simplicity our whole appearance is franker, more natural.
This true simplicity...makes us conscious of a certain openness, gentleness, innocence, gaiety,
and serenity, which is charming when we see it near to and continually, with pure eyes.*

FRANÇOIS FÉNELON

Childlike Simplicity

Recently my sister, Ann, and I spent a whole day "going back in time" and looking for the two little blonde-haired girls we used to be. Our nostalgic journey took us back to our old neighborhood. There was our old house—with a slight face-lift and a bold new paint job, but still our old house.

The new homeowner was a little suspicious at first when she saw us hanging about, but after we explained who we were she ended up asking us inside. We went from room to room, whispering and giggling and feeling like kids, letting each room recall another memory and each memory another story. Most of the house had been remodeled, but a few things had not been changed. The molding around the floors and ceiling and fireplace was the

way we remembered it. The knotty pine paneling in the den had been painted over, but the knots were still there! The tile in the bathroom was exactly the same.

Then something amazing hit me like a ton of bricks, right in the middle of all the emotion and all the memories. I realized that even under all this remodeling, it really was still the same house! These were the same floors we had

walked around on, the same windows we had looked out of growing up. But more than that, it also hit me that under all of our grown-up clothes and our makeup and our education and experiences, Ann and I were still the same little girls—the same little tow-headed, mischievous kids who had grown up here all those years ago.

I was suddenly filled with a warmth and love not only for my little sister, but (strangely) for myself as a child. I was deeply touched by the innocence and hope and vulnerability we had possessed as children, and I recognized its value.

Traveling in the company of those we love is home in motion.

LEIGH HUNT

All-Encompassing Joy

One of the reasons we adults like to take children to amusement parks is that children give us permission to enter into the joy of the moment. But it certainly doesn't take a big, shiny theme park to delight a little child. Something small can bring enormous pleasure to a child's heart. Have you ever noticed a baby on Christmas morning? While the adults are exclaiming over the gifts, baby's over in the corner delighting in the cast-off wrapping paper!

On a recent canoe trip to North Carolina with friends, Spike was strengthened and buoyed by the childlike joy of a wonderful moment. Here is how he recorded it in his journal:

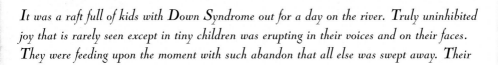

Somewhere near the beginning of my river run, while I was still fine-tuning my paddling technique and becoming comfortable with the river and its forces, I heard behind me a joyous tumult of laughter from an oncoming raft…I turned just in time to see a large raft filled to overflowing with madly paddling youngsters, all of them in full-throated laughter.

It was a raft full of kids with Down Syndrome out for a day on the river. Truly uninhibited joy that is rarely seen except in tiny children was erupting in their voices and on their faces. They were feeding upon the moment with such abandon that all else was swept away. Their

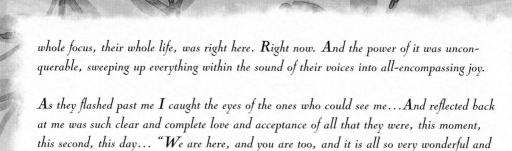

whole focus, their whole life, was right here. *Right* now. *And* the power of it was unconquerable, sweeping up everything within the sound of their voices into all-encompassing joy.

As they flashed past me *I* caught the eyes of the ones who could see me...*And* reflected back at me was such clear and complete love and acceptance of all that they were, this moment, this second, this day... *"We* are here, and you are too, and it is all so very wonderful and grand and not to be contained," their eyes seemed to say as they swept past me, laughing and shouting and splashing their paddles and bouncing down the current and around the bend.

Laughter is the music of life.

SIR WILLIAM OSLER

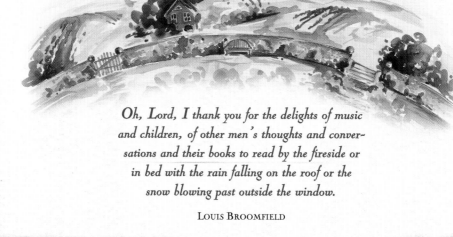

*Oh, Lord, I thank you for the delights of music
and children, of other men's thoughts and conversations and their books to read by the fireside or
in bed with the rain falling on the roof or the
snow blowing past outside the window.*

LOUIS BROOMFIELD

Precious
Child

Where is that girl that you used to be,
The one with the bruises and scrapes on her
knee,
The one who wore feelings and faith on her sleeve –
Where is that precious child?

Where is that boy who loved a surprise,
Who had pockets of wishes and dreams in his eyes,
Who loved to make pictures of clouds in the skies –
Where is that precious child?

How did all the work and worry
Bury the hope and the trust?
Listen to Jesus; He's calling us back,
Back to the child in us.

Where is that child that yesterday knew?
Where are those feelings so simple and true?
Jesus is beckoning me and you
Back to that precious child.
Lord, take me back to that precious child.

CLAIRE CLONINGER

Very little is needed to make a happy life.

MARCUS AURELIUS